Karine-Marie Amiot & Lucie Minne

Where Are You From?

The Wonderful Story of Your Birth

In the beginning,
before your parents ever imagined you,
God wanted you to be born.

One beautiful day,
your mom and dad met and fell in love.
They soon started dreaming of a beautiful child… you.

They loved each other very much.
One day, you arrived in your mother's belly.
God saw and knew it was good.

You were smaller than a grain of sand
and invisible to the naked eye.
You were so small that only God knew you were there.

God's voice was able to reach you. God said,
"My child, my little one, I love you."

The sun went down and rose again
on a new day, full of promise.

And then, warm and snug,
like a chick in a nest,
you started to grow.
Slowly. At your own pace.

When your parents learned that you
were there, they were filled with love for you,
even though they couldn't see you.
They imagined what you'd be like… you,
their beloved baby…

"Thank you!"
Their words of gratitude rose up to God,
who was tirelessly watching over the three of you.

They celebrated all evening.
And then it was night.

A new day began.
Another special day!

Your heart started to beat,
for life,
for your entire life…
"You will have a beautiful baby!" God said.

That day came to an end and a new day began.

Two legs, to run like the wind…
two hands and ten fingers, to draw and invent and explore—
you already had all of those things!

That day came to an end and a new day began,
and God never tired of looking at your beautiful face.
Your nose. Your mouth.
God thought you were perfect. Magnificent.
One of a kind!

God saw that it was all good—very, very good.

That day came to an end and a new day began.

A girl?
Or a boy?
There could be no wrong answer.
Girl or boy, it would be you.

In your little hiding place, you started to move and swim like a fish.

Then that day came to an end and a new day began.

You loved hearing your mom's heartbeat.

With your thumb in your mouth,
you listened closely to hear
your dad's voice, his laugh and his loving words.

The day came to an end and a new day began.

Between somersaults,
you were getting ready.

You were saving your strength to be born,
because you were starting to feel cramped
and were eager to meet the world.

You had been growing there, patiently,
for nine months.

You were looking forward to seeing the sky, the sun,
the trees, the flowers,
the moon, the stars,
and your parents' faces.

One morning,
after a long night,
you finally arrived.

And God smiled.

Originally published by Fleurus MAME

First edition published 2016
Printed in USA
22 21 20 19 18 17 16   1 2 3 4 5 6 7 8
ISBN: 978-1-5064-1864-3

Library of Congress Cataloging-in-Publication Data is available

Sparkhouse Family
510 Marquette Avenue
Minneapolis, MN 55402
sparkhouse.org